50 Premium Holiday Bread Recipes

By: Kelly Johnson

Table of Contents

- Classic Holiday Fruit Bread
- Cinnamon Swirl Christmas Bread
- Cranberry Orange Nut Bread
- Pumpkin Spice Brioche
- Gingerbread Loaf
- Eggnog Brioche
- Pecan Sticky Buns
- Sweet Potato Cinnamon Rolls
- Almond Crescent Rolls
- Maple Walnut Dinner Rolls
- Holiday Poppy Seed Bread
- Saffron Brioche
- Chocolate Hazelnut Babka
- Cranberry Pistachio Loaf
- Lemon-Glazed Gingerbread Cake
- Apricot and Almond Brioche
- Caramelized Onion and Gruyère Bread
- Rustic Rosemary Olive Bread
- Apple Cinnamon Pull-Apart Bread
- Festive Stollen with Marzipan
- Walnut Sage Focaccia
- Pear and Cardamom Bread
- Cardamom and Cinnamon Bread Rolls
- Orange and Poppy Seed Cake
- Cranberry Walnut Sourdough
- Spiced Apricot Breakfast Bread
- Fig and Pistachio Challah
- Zesty Lemon-Blueberry Cake Bread
- Cranberry Almond Scones
- Pear and Gingerbread Quick Bread
- Rustic Chestnut Bread
- Maple Cinnamon Rolls
- Nutmeg and Honey Whole Wheat Bread
- Bourbon-Soaked Fruit Bread
- Egg-Free Christmas Stollen

- Chocolate Chip Babka with Pistachios
- Pumpkin Pecan Bread
- Banana Nut Bread with Bourbon
- Holiday Spice Hot Cross Buns
- White Chocolate Cranberry Loaf
- Cinnamon Sugar Pull-Apart Bread
- Cranberry Apple Cinnamon Streusel Bread
- Pistachio and Apricot Panettone
- Ginger-Spiced Pear Bread
- Buttery Sweet Potato Bread
- Red Velvet Pound Cake
- Sweet Sourdough Fruit Loaf
- Poppy Seed Swiss Roll
- Mulled Wine Bread
- Citrus Walnut Bread

Classic Holiday Fruit Bread

Ingredients:

- 3 cups all-purpose flour
- 1/2 cup sugar
- 1/2 teaspoon salt
- 1 packet active dry yeast
- 1/2 cup warm water
- 1/2 cup milk
- 1/2 cup unsalted butter, softened
- 2 large eggs
- 1 cup mixed dried fruit (raisins, cranberries, chopped apricots)
- 1/2 cup chopped nuts (walnuts, almonds, or pecans)
- 1 teaspoon cinnamon
- 1/2 teaspoon nutmeg

Instructions:

1. **Prepare the dough**: In a large bowl, combine flour, sugar, salt, and yeast. In a separate bowl, warm the water and milk together, then add the butter, eggs, and spices. Gradually mix in the wet ingredients with the dry ingredients to form a dough.
2. **Knead**: Turn the dough out onto a floured surface and knead for about 10 minutes, until smooth. Add the dried fruit and nuts during the last few minutes of kneading.
3. **Rise**: Place the dough in a greased bowl, cover with a clean cloth, and let it rise in a warm place for 1 hour or until doubled in size.
4. **Shape and bake**: Punch the dough down, shape it into a loaf, and place it in a greased loaf pan. Let it rise for another 30 minutes. Preheat the oven to 350°F (175°C) and bake for 30-35 minutes, or until golden brown.
5. **Serve**: Cool before slicing.

Cinnamon Swirl Christmas Bread

Ingredients:

- 3 cups all-purpose flour
- 1/4 cup sugar
- 1 packet active dry yeast
- 1 teaspoon cinnamon
- 1/2 teaspoon salt
- 1/2 cup warm milk
- 1/4 cup warm water
- 2 tablespoons unsalted butter, softened
- 1 large egg
- 1/2 cup brown sugar
- 1 tablespoon cinnamon (for swirl)

Instructions:

1. **Prepare the dough**: In a bowl, combine the flour, sugar, yeast, cinnamon, and salt. In another bowl, combine warm milk, warm water, butter, and egg. Gradually add the wet ingredients to the dry ingredients and knead until a smooth dough forms.
2. **Rise**: Cover the dough with a cloth and let it rise for 1 hour.
3. **Shape and swirl**: Roll the dough into a rectangle. Mix brown sugar and cinnamon for the swirl, and sprinkle it evenly over the dough. Roll it up tightly and place it in a greased loaf pan.
4. **Bake**: Preheat oven to 350°F (175°C) and bake for 25-30 minutes, until golden.
5. **Serve**: Cool slightly before slicing.

Cranberry Orange Nut Bread

Ingredients:

- 2 cups all-purpose flour
- 1 tablespoon baking powder
- 1/2 teaspoon baking soda
- 1/2 teaspoon salt
- 1 cup sugar
- 2 large eggs
- 1/2 cup orange juice
- 1/4 cup unsalted butter, melted
- 1 teaspoon vanilla extract
- 1 cup fresh cranberries, chopped
- 1/2 cup chopped walnuts

Instructions:

1. **Mix dry ingredients**: In a bowl, combine flour, baking powder, baking soda, salt, and sugar.
2. **Combine wet ingredients**: In another bowl, whisk together eggs, orange juice, butter, and vanilla extract.
3. **Combine wet and dry**: Pour the wet ingredients into the dry ingredients and stir until just combined. Gently fold in cranberries and walnuts.
4. **Bake**: Preheat the oven to 350°F (175°C). Pour the batter into a greased loaf pan and bake for 55-60 minutes.
5. **Serve**: Let it cool before slicing.

Pumpkin Spice Brioche

Ingredients:

- 3 cups all-purpose flour
- 1/4 cup sugar
- 1 packet active dry yeast
- 1 teaspoon pumpkin pie spice
- 1/2 teaspoon salt
- 1/2 cup warm milk
- 1/4 cup unsalted butter, softened
- 2 large eggs
- 1 cup pumpkin puree

Instructions:

1. **Prepare the dough**: Combine flour, sugar, yeast, pumpkin pie spice, and salt in a bowl. In another bowl, combine warm milk, butter, eggs, and pumpkin puree. Gradually mix the wet ingredients into the dry ingredients.
2. **Knead**: Knead the dough for 10 minutes until smooth. Place it in a greased bowl, cover, and let it rise for 1 hour.
3. **Shape and bake**: Punch the dough down, shape it into a loaf, and place it in a greased loaf pan. Let it rise for another 30 minutes. Preheat the oven to 350°F (175°C) and bake for 30-35 minutes.
4. **Serve**: Let it cool before slicing.

Gingerbread Loaf

Ingredients:

- 2 1/2 cups all-purpose flour
- 1 teaspoon baking powder
- 1/2 teaspoon baking soda
- 1/2 teaspoon salt
- 1 teaspoon ground ginger
- 1 teaspoon ground cinnamon
- 1/4 teaspoon ground cloves
- 1/2 cup unsalted butter, softened
- 1/2 cup brown sugar
- 2 large eggs
- 1 cup molasses
- 1/2 cup hot water

Instructions:

1. **Prepare the dry ingredients**: In a bowl, whisk together flour, baking powder, baking soda, salt, ginger, cinnamon, and cloves.
2. **Make the batter**: In another bowl, beat the butter and sugar until light and fluffy. Add the eggs and molasses and mix well. Gradually add the dry ingredients and hot water, mixing until smooth.
3. **Bake**: Preheat oven to 350°F (175°C). Pour the batter into a greased loaf pan and bake for 50-55 minutes, or until a toothpick comes out clean.
4. **Serve**: Let it cool before slicing.

Eggnog Brioche

Ingredients:

- 3 cups all-purpose flour
- 1/2 cup sugar
- 1 packet active dry yeast
- 1/2 teaspoon salt
- 1/2 teaspoon ground nutmeg
- 1/4 teaspoon ground cinnamon
- 1/2 cup eggnog
- 1/2 cup unsalted butter, softened
- 4 large eggs
- 1/4 cup milk
- 1 tablespoon vanilla extract

Instructions:

1. **Prepare the dough**: In a bowl, combine flour, sugar, yeast, salt, nutmeg, and cinnamon. In another bowl, whisk together eggnog, butter, eggs, milk, and vanilla. Gradually combine the wet and dry ingredients, mixing until a dough forms.
2. **Knead**: Knead the dough for 10-12 minutes until smooth and elastic. Place in a greased bowl, cover, and let rise for 1 hour.
3. **Shape and bake**: Punch the dough down and shape it into a loaf. Place it in a greased loaf pan and let it rise for another 30 minutes. Preheat oven to 350°F (175°C) and bake for 25-30 minutes.
4. **Serve**: Let the bread cool before slicing.

Pecan Sticky Buns

Ingredients:

- 2 1/2 cups all-purpose flour
- 1 packet active dry yeast
- 1/2 cup milk, warmed
- 1/4 cup sugar
- 1/2 teaspoon salt
- 1/4 cup unsalted butter, softened
- 2 large eggs
- 1 cup chopped pecans
- 1/2 cup brown sugar
- 1/2 cup unsalted butter, melted
- 1 tablespoon cinnamon

Instructions:

1. **Prepare the dough**: In a bowl, combine flour, yeast, warm milk, sugar, salt, butter, and eggs. Mix until a dough forms. Knead for 8-10 minutes, then cover and let rise for 1 hour.
2. **Make the filling**: In a bowl, combine brown sugar, cinnamon, and melted butter.
3. **Shape and bake**: Roll the dough into a rectangle and spread the filling evenly. Sprinkle with chopped pecans and roll up the dough. Slice into individual buns and place them in a greased baking dish. Let them rise for 30 minutes.
4. **Bake**: Preheat oven to 350°F (175°C) and bake for 25-30 minutes, until golden brown.
5. **Serve**: Drizzle with additional melted butter and serve warm.

Sweet Potato Cinnamon Rolls

Ingredients:

- 3 cups all-purpose flour
- 1 packet active dry yeast
- 1/2 cup warm milk
- 1/4 cup sugar
- 1/2 teaspoon salt
- 1/4 cup unsalted butter, softened
- 1 large egg
- 1 cup mashed sweet potato
- 1/4 cup brown sugar
- 1 tablespoon cinnamon

Instructions:

1. **Prepare the dough**: In a bowl, combine flour, yeast, warm milk, sugar, salt, butter, egg, and mashed sweet potato. Mix until a dough forms. Knead for 8-10 minutes, then cover and let rise for 1 hour.
2. **Make the filling**: In a bowl, mix brown sugar and cinnamon.
3. **Shape and bake**: Roll the dough into a rectangle and spread the cinnamon-sugar mixture over it. Roll up the dough and slice into individual rolls. Place them in a greased baking dish and let rise for 30 minutes.
4. **Bake**: Preheat oven to 350°F (175°C) and bake for 25-30 minutes, until golden brown.
5. **Serve**: Drizzle with icing or serve warm.

Almond Crescent Rolls

Ingredients:

- 3 cups all-purpose flour
- 1 packet active dry yeast
- 1/2 cup warm milk
- 1/4 cup sugar
- 1/2 teaspoon salt
- 1/2 cup unsalted butter, softened
- 2 large eggs
- 1 teaspoon almond extract
- 1/2 cup chopped almonds

Instructions:

1. **Prepare the dough**: In a bowl, combine flour, yeast, warm milk, sugar, salt, butter, eggs, and almond extract. Mix until smooth. Knead for 8-10 minutes and let the dough rise for 1 hour.
2. **Shape and bake**: Roll the dough into a circle and cut it into wedges. Roll each wedge up into a crescent shape. Place them on a baking sheet and let rise for 30 minutes.
3. **Bake**: Preheat oven to 375°F (190°C) and bake for 15-18 minutes, until golden brown.
4. **Serve**: Cool before serving.

Maple Walnut Dinner Rolls

Ingredients:

- 3 cups all-purpose flour
- 1 packet active dry yeast
- 1/4 cup sugar
- 1/2 teaspoon salt
- 1/2 cup warm milk
- 1/4 cup unsalted butter, softened
- 2 large eggs
- 1/2 cup chopped walnuts
- 2 tablespoons maple syrup

Instructions:

1. **Prepare the dough**: Combine flour, yeast, sugar, and salt in a bowl. In another bowl, combine warm milk, butter, eggs, and maple syrup. Gradually mix in the wet ingredients with the dry ingredients.
2. **Knead**: Knead the dough until smooth, then place it in a greased bowl, cover, and let rise for 1 hour.
3. **Shape and bake**: Punch the dough down and shape it into rolls. Place the rolls on a greased baking sheet and sprinkle with chopped walnuts. Let rise for 30 minutes.
4. **Bake**: Preheat oven to 375°F (190°C) and bake for 18-20 minutes.
5. **Serve**: Let the rolls cool before serving.

Holiday Poppy Seed Bread

Ingredients:

- 2 cups all-purpose flour
- 1 packet active dry yeast
- 1/2 teaspoon salt
- 1/2 cup sugar
- 1 cup warm milk
- 1/4 cup unsalted butter, softened
- 2 large eggs
- 1/4 cup poppy seeds

Instructions:

1. **Prepare the dough**: Combine flour, yeast, salt, and sugar in a bowl. In another bowl, combine warm milk, butter, eggs, and poppy seeds. Gradually mix in the wet ingredients with the dry ingredients.
2. **Knead**: Knead the dough for 8-10 minutes, then let it rise in a greased bowl for 1 hour.
3. **Shape and bake**: Punch the dough down and shape it into a loaf. Place in a greased loaf pan and let rise for another 30 minutes.
4. **Bake**: Preheat oven to 350°F (175°C) and bake for 25-30 minutes.
5. **Serve**: Cool before slicing.

Saffron Brioche

Ingredients:

- 3 cups all-purpose flour
- 1 packet active dry yeast
- 1/4 cup sugar
- 1/2 teaspoon salt
- 1/2 teaspoon saffron threads, crushed
- 1/2 cup warm milk
- 1/2 cup unsalted butter, softened
- 3 large eggs
- 1/2 cup heavy cream
- 1 teaspoon vanilla extract

Instructions:

1. **Prepare the dough**: In a bowl, combine flour, yeast, sugar, salt, and saffron. In a separate bowl, whisk together warm milk, butter, eggs, cream, and vanilla. Gradually mix the wet ingredients into the dry ingredients, and knead the dough for 10 minutes.
2. **Let rise**: Place the dough in a greased bowl, cover with a cloth, and let it rise for 1-2 hours until doubled in size.
3. **Shape and bake**: Punch down the dough and shape it into a loaf. Let it rise for another 30 minutes. Preheat oven to 350°F (175°C). Bake for 25-30 minutes, until golden brown.
4. **Serve**: Let the brioche cool before serving.

Chocolate Hazelnut Babka

Ingredients:

- 3 cups all-purpose flour
- 1 packet active dry yeast
- 1/2 cup sugar
- 1/2 teaspoon salt
- 1/2 cup warm milk
- 1/2 cup unsalted butter, softened
- 3 large eggs
- 1/2 cup hazelnut spread
- 1/4 cup chopped hazelnuts
- 1/4 cup cocoa powder
- 1 tablespoon vanilla extract

Instructions:

1. **Prepare the dough**: In a bowl, combine flour, yeast, sugar, and salt. In another bowl, whisk together warm milk, butter, eggs, and vanilla. Gradually add the wet ingredients to the dry and knead until smooth. Let the dough rise for 1 hour.
2. **Shape and fill**: Roll the dough into a rectangle. Spread hazelnut spread and cocoa powder evenly over the dough, then sprinkle with chopped hazelnuts. Roll up the dough and slice it in half, twisting the two pieces together into a loaf.
3. **Bake**: Preheat oven to 350°F (175°C) and bake for 30-35 minutes, until golden brown and cooked through.
4. **Serve**: Cool slightly before slicing.

Cranberry Pistachio Loaf

Ingredients:

- 2 1/2 cups all-purpose flour
- 1 packet active dry yeast
- 1/2 cup sugar
- 1/2 teaspoon salt
- 1/2 cup warm water
- 1/4 cup unsalted butter, melted
- 1 large egg
- 1 cup dried cranberries
- 1/2 cup pistachios, chopped

Instructions:

1. **Prepare the dough**: In a bowl, combine flour, yeast, sugar, and salt. In another bowl, mix warm water, melted butter, and egg. Gradually combine the wet and dry ingredients, then knead the dough for 8-10 minutes.
2. **Let rise**: Place the dough in a greased bowl and let it rise for 1 hour.
3. **Add cranberries and pistachios**: Punch down the dough and fold in cranberries and pistachios. Shape the dough into a loaf and place it in a greased pan. Let it rise for another 30 minutes.
4. **Bake**: Preheat oven to 350°F (175°C) and bake for 25-30 minutes, until golden.
5. **Serve**: Let the loaf cool before serving.

Lemon-Glazed Gingerbread Cake

Ingredients:

- 2 cups all-purpose flour
- 1 teaspoon ground ginger
- 1 teaspoon ground cinnamon
- 1/2 teaspoon ground cloves
- 1/2 teaspoon baking soda
- 1/2 teaspoon salt
- 1/2 cup unsalted butter, softened
- 1 cup molasses
- 1/2 cup sugar
- 2 large eggs
- 1/2 cup hot water
- 1 tablespoon lemon zest
- 1/4 cup lemon juice
- 1/2 cup powdered sugar

Instructions:

1. **Prepare the cake**: Preheat oven to 350°F (175°C). Grease and flour a cake pan. In a bowl, combine flour, spices, baking soda, and salt. In another bowl, beat together butter, molasses, sugar, and eggs. Gradually add the dry ingredients and hot water, mixing until smooth.
2. **Bake**: Pour the batter into the prepared pan and bake for 30-35 minutes, until a toothpick comes out clean.
3. **Make the glaze**: In a small bowl, mix lemon juice, zest, and powdered sugar to make the glaze.
4. **Serve**: Drizzle the glaze over the cooled cake before serving.

Apricot and Almond Brioche

Ingredients:

- 3 cups all-purpose flour
- 1 packet active dry yeast
- 1/4 cup sugar
- 1/2 teaspoon salt
- 1/2 cup warm milk
- 1/2 cup unsalted butter, softened
- 3 large eggs
- 1 cup dried apricots, chopped
- 1/2 cup sliced almonds

Instructions:

1. **Prepare the dough**: In a bowl, combine flour, yeast, sugar, and salt. In another bowl, whisk together warm milk, butter, eggs, and mix well. Gradually combine the wet and dry ingredients, kneading until smooth. Let the dough rise for 1-2 hours.
2. **Add apricots and almonds**: Punch down the dough and fold in apricots and almonds. Shape the dough into a loaf and let it rise for another 30 minutes.
3. **Bake**: Preheat oven to 350°F (175°C) and bake for 25-30 minutes, until golden brown.
4. **Serve**: Cool before slicing.

Caramelized Onion and Gruyère Bread

Ingredients:

- 3 cups all-purpose flour
- 1 packet active dry yeast
- 1/2 cup warm water
- 1 tablespoon sugar
- 1 teaspoon salt
- 1/4 cup olive oil
- 1 large onion, caramelized
- 1 cup grated Gruyère cheese

Instructions:

1. **Prepare the dough**: In a bowl, combine flour, yeast, sugar, and salt. In another bowl, mix warm water and olive oil. Gradually combine the wet and dry ingredients, then knead for 8-10 minutes. Let the dough rise for 1 hour.
2. **Add onion and cheese**: Punch down the dough and fold in caramelized onions and grated Gruyère. Shape the dough into a loaf and let it rise for another 30 minutes.
3. **Bake**: Preheat oven to 375°F (190°C) and bake for 30-35 minutes, until golden.
4. **Serve**: Cool before slicing.

Rustic Rosemary Olive Bread

Ingredients:

- 3 cups all-purpose flour
- 1 packet active dry yeast
- 1/2 teaspoon salt
- 1/2 cup warm water
- 2 tablespoons olive oil
- 1/4 cup chopped fresh rosemary
- 1/2 cup black olives, pitted and chopped

Instructions:

1. **Prepare the dough**: In a bowl, combine flour, yeast, and salt. Gradually add warm water and olive oil, mixing to form a dough. Knead for 8-10 minutes, then let rise for 1 hour.
2. **Add rosemary and olives**: Punch down the dough and fold in chopped rosemary and olives. Shape into a loaf and let it rise for another 30 minutes.
3. **Bake**: Preheat oven to 375°F (190°C) and bake for 25-30 minutes, until golden brown.
4. **Serve**: Cool before serving.

Apple Cinnamon Pull-Apart Bread

Ingredients:

- 3 cups all-purpose flour
- 1 packet active dry yeast
- 1/2 cup sugar
- 1/2 teaspoon salt
- 1/2 cup warm milk
- 1/4 cup unsalted butter, melted
- 2 large apples, peeled and chopped
- 1 tablespoon cinnamon

Instructions:

1. **Prepare the dough**: In a bowl, combine flour, yeast, sugar, and salt. Gradually add warm milk and melted butter, mixing until smooth. Knead for 8-10 minutes, then let rise for 1 hour.
2. **Shape and fill**: Roll the dough into a rectangle and sprinkle with chopped apples and cinnamon. Slice into strips and stack them, then cut the stack into squares. Arrange them in a greased pan and let rise for 30 minutes.
3. **Bake**: Preheat oven to 350°F (175°C) and bake for 30-35 minutes.
4. **Serve**: Cool before serving.

Festive Stollen with Marzipan

Ingredients:

- 4 cups all-purpose flour
- 1 packet active dry yeast
- 1/2 teaspoon salt
- 1/2 cup sugar
- 1/2 cup warm milk
- 1/2 cup unsalted butter, softened
- 1/2 cup marzipan, rolled into a log
- 1 cup mixed dried fruit
- 1 teaspoon cinnamon
- Powdered sugar, for dusting

Instructions:

1. **Prepare the dough**: In a bowl, combine flour, yeast, salt, and sugar. Add warm milk and butter, mixing until smooth. Let the dough rise for 1 hour.
2. **Shape the stollen**: Roll the dough into a rectangle, place the marzipan log in the center, and fold the dough over. Shape into a loaf and let rise for another hour.
3. **Bake**: Preheat oven to 350°F (175°C) and bake for 30-35 minutes.
4. **Serve**: Dust with powdered sugar and slice before serving.

Walnut Sage Focaccia

Ingredients:

- 3 cups all-purpose flour
- 1 packet active dry yeast
- 1/2 teaspoon salt
- 1 cup warm water
- 2 tablespoons olive oil
- 1/4 cup chopped walnuts
- 2 tablespoons fresh sage, chopped

Instructions:

1. **Prepare the dough**: In a bowl, combine flour, yeast, and salt. Add warm water and olive oil, mixing to form a dough. Knead for 10 minutes, then let rise for 1 hour.
2. **Shape the focaccia**: Roll the dough onto a baking sheet and press down with your fingers. Sprinkle with walnuts and sage. Let rise for 30 minutes.
3. **Bake**: Preheat oven to 375°F (190°C) and bake for 20-25 minutes, until golden.
4. **Serve**: Cool before slicing.

Pear and Cardamom Bread

Ingredients:

- 2 1/2 cups all-purpose flour
- 1 packet active dry yeast
- 1/2 teaspoon salt
- 1/2 teaspoon ground cardamom
- 1/2 cup sugar
- 1/2 cup warm milk
- 1/4 cup unsalted butter, melted
- 1 large pear, peeled and chopped

Instructions:

1. **Prepare the dough**: In a bowl, combine flour, yeast, salt, cardamom, and sugar. Gradually add warm milk and melted butter, mixing to form a dough. Knead for 8-10 minutes.
2. **Shape and rise**: Fold in chopped pear and shape into a loaf. Let it rise for 1 hour.
3. **Bake**: Preheat oven to 350°F (175°C) and bake for 30-35 minutes.
4. **Serve**: Cool before serving.

Cardamom and Cinnamon Bread Rolls

Ingredients:

- 3 cups all-purpose flour
- 1 packet active dry yeast
- 1/2 cup sugar
- 1/2 teaspoon salt
- 1/2 teaspoon ground cardamom
- 1/2 teaspoon ground cinnamon
- 1/2 cup warm milk
- 1/2 cup unsalted butter, melted

Instructions:

1. **Prepare the dough**: In a bowl, combine flour, yeast, sugar, salt, cardamom, and cinnamon. Add warm milk and melted butter, mixing to form a dough. Knead for 8-10 minutes and let it rise for 1 hour.
2. **Shape the rolls**: Roll the dough into small balls and place them on a baking sheet. Let them rise for 30 minutes.
3. **Bake**: Preheat oven to 350°F (175°C) and bake for 15-20 minutes, until golden.
4. **Serve**: Cool slightly before serving.

Orange and Poppy Seed Cake

Ingredients:

- 2 cups all-purpose flour
- 1 tablespoon poppy seeds
- 1 teaspoon baking powder
- 1/2 teaspoon baking soda
- 1/2 teaspoon salt
- 1/2 cup unsalted butter, softened
- 1 cup sugar
- 3 large eggs
- 1/2 cup sour cream
- 1/4 cup freshly squeezed orange juice
- Zest of 1 orange
- 1 teaspoon vanilla extract

Instructions:

1. **Preheat the oven**: Preheat oven to 350°F (175°C) and grease a 9-inch round cake pan.
2. **Prepare the dry ingredients**: In a bowl, mix flour, poppy seeds, baking powder, baking soda, and salt.
3. **Cream the butter and sugar**: In another bowl, beat butter and sugar until light and fluffy. Add eggs, one at a time, beating well after each addition.
4. **Add the wet ingredients**: Stir in sour cream, orange juice, orange zest, and vanilla extract.
5. **Combine**: Gradually add the dry ingredients, mixing until just combined.
6. **Bake**: Pour the batter into the prepared pan and bake for 30-35 minutes, or until a toothpick comes out clean.
7. **Serve**: Let cool before serving.

Cranberry Walnut Sourdough

Ingredients:

- 3 cups all-purpose flour
- 1/2 cup whole wheat flour
- 1 teaspoon salt
- 1 cup sourdough starter
- 1/2 cup warm water
- 1/2 cup dried cranberries
- 1/2 cup walnuts, chopped
- 1 tablespoon honey

Instructions:

1. **Make the dough**: In a large bowl, mix the flours and salt. Add sourdough starter, warm water, and honey. Mix to form a dough.
2. **Knead the dough**: Turn the dough onto a floured surface and knead for 8-10 minutes, adding cranberries and walnuts halfway through.
3. **First rise**: Place the dough in a lightly greased bowl, cover, and let rise for 3-4 hours, or until doubled in size.
4. **Shape and second rise**: Shape the dough into a loaf and place it on a parchment-lined baking sheet. Let rise for another 1-2 hours.
5. **Bake**: Preheat oven to 450°F (230°C). Bake for 35-40 minutes, until golden and crusty.
6. **Serve**: Cool before slicing.

Spiced Apricot Breakfast Bread

Ingredients:

- 2 cups all-purpose flour
- 1 teaspoon baking powder
- 1/2 teaspoon baking soda
- 1/2 teaspoon cinnamon
- 1/4 teaspoon ground ginger
- 1/4 teaspoon nutmeg
- 1/2 cup unsalted butter, softened
- 1 cup brown sugar
- 2 large eggs
- 1 cup dried apricots, chopped
- 1/2 cup yogurt
- 1/4 cup milk
- 1 teaspoon vanilla extract

Instructions:

1. **Preheat the oven**: Preheat the oven to 350°F (175°C) and grease a loaf pan.
2. **Prepare the dry ingredients**: In a bowl, combine flour, baking powder, baking soda, cinnamon, ginger, and nutmeg.
3. **Cream the butter and sugar**: Beat butter and brown sugar until light and fluffy. Add eggs, one at a time, beating well.
4. **Add the wet ingredients**: Stir in yogurt, milk, and vanilla.
5. **Combine**: Gradually mix in the dry ingredients. Fold in chopped apricots.
6. **Bake**: Pour batter into the loaf pan and bake for 45-50 minutes, or until golden and a toothpick comes out clean.
7. **Serve**: Let cool before serving.

Fig and Pistachio Challah

Ingredients:

- 3 1/2 cups all-purpose flour
- 1/4 cup sugar
- 1 packet active dry yeast
- 1 teaspoon salt
- 1/4 cup warm water
- 1/2 cup milk
- 1/2 cup unsalted butter, melted
- 2 large eggs
- 1/2 cup dried figs, chopped
- 1/4 cup pistachios, chopped
- 1 egg (for egg wash)

Instructions:

1. **Prepare the dough**: In a bowl, combine flour, sugar, yeast, and salt. Add warm water, milk, butter, and eggs. Mix to form a dough.
2. **Knead the dough**: Turn the dough onto a floured surface and knead for 8-10 minutes. Add figs and pistachios and knead until incorporated.
3. **First rise**: Place dough in a greased bowl, cover, and let rise for 1-2 hours, until doubled.
4. **Shape the challah**: Punch down the dough and divide into 3 sections. Roll each section into ropes and braid them together. Let rise for 1 hour.
5. **Bake**: Preheat oven to 375°F (190°C). Brush the bread with egg wash and bake for 25-30 minutes, until golden.
6. **Serve**: Let cool before slicing.

Zesty Lemon-Blueberry Cake Bread

Ingredients:

- 2 cups all-purpose flour
- 1 teaspoon baking powder
- 1/2 teaspoon salt
- 1 cup sugar
- 1/2 cup unsalted butter, softened
- 2 large eggs
- 1/2 cup milk
- Zest of 1 lemon
- 1 1/2 cups fresh blueberries
- 1 tablespoon lemon juice

Instructions:

1. **Preheat the oven**: Preheat the oven to 350°F (175°C) and grease a loaf pan.
2. **Prepare the dry ingredients**: In a bowl, combine flour, baking powder, and salt.
3. **Cream the butter and sugar**: Beat butter and sugar until light and fluffy. Add eggs, one at a time.
4. **Add the wet ingredients**: Stir in milk, lemon zest, and lemon juice.
5. **Combine**: Gradually mix in the dry ingredients. Fold in blueberries.
6. **Bake**: Pour batter into the loaf pan and bake for 50-55 minutes, until golden and a toothpick comes out clean.
7. **Serve**: Cool before slicing.

Cranberry Almond Scones

Ingredients:

- 2 cups all-purpose flour
- 1/4 cup sugar
- 1 tablespoon baking powder
- 1/4 teaspoon salt
- 1/2 cup unsalted butter, chilled and cut into cubes
- 1/2 cup dried cranberries
- 1/4 cup sliced almonds
- 2/3 cup heavy cream
- 1 teaspoon vanilla extract

Instructions:

1. **Preheat the oven**: Preheat the oven to 400°F (200°C) and line a baking sheet with parchment paper.
2. **Prepare the dry ingredients**: In a bowl, combine flour, sugar, baking powder, and salt.
3. **Cut in the butter**: Add chilled butter and cut it into the flour mixture using a pastry cutter until it resembles coarse crumbs.
4. **Add cranberries and almonds**: Stir in cranberries and almonds.
5. **Form the dough**: Stir in heavy cream and vanilla, then mix until just combined.
6. **Shape and bake**: Pat the dough into a circle and cut into 8 wedges. Bake for 15-18 minutes, until golden.
7. **Serve**: Cool slightly before serving.

Pear and Gingerbread Quick Bread

Ingredients:

- 1 1/2 cups all-purpose flour
- 1 teaspoon baking soda
- 1 teaspoon ground cinnamon
- 1/2 teaspoon ground ginger
- 1/4 teaspoon ground cloves
- 1/4 teaspoon ground nutmeg
- 1/2 teaspoon salt
- 1/2 cup unsalted butter, softened
- 3/4 cup brown sugar
- 2 large eggs
- 1 cup pear puree (or mashed pears)
- 1/2 cup milk
- 1 teaspoon vanilla extract
- 1/2 cup chopped pecans or walnuts (optional)

Instructions:

1. **Preheat the oven:** Preheat the oven to 350°F (175°C). Grease and flour a loaf pan.
2. **Mix dry ingredients:** In a bowl, whisk together flour, baking soda, spices, and salt.
3. **Cream the butter and sugar:** Beat butter and brown sugar until light and fluffy. Add eggs one at a time, mixing well between each.
4. **Add wet ingredients:** Stir in pear puree, milk, and vanilla extract.
5. **Combine and bake:** Gradually add the dry ingredients to the wet mixture and stir until just combined. Fold in nuts if using.
6. **Bake:** Pour the batter into the prepared loaf pan and bake for 50-60 minutes, or until a toothpick inserted in the center comes out clean.
7. **Cool and serve:** Allow the bread to cool before slicing.

Rustic Chestnut Bread

Ingredients:

- 2 cups chestnut flour
- 1 cup all-purpose flour
- 1 teaspoon salt
- 1 teaspoon active dry yeast
- 1 tablespoon olive oil
- 1 1/4 cups warm water
- 1 tablespoon honey
- 1 tablespoon fresh rosemary, chopped (optional)

Instructions:

1. **Prepare the yeast:** In a bowl, combine warm water, honey, and yeast. Let sit for 5-10 minutes until frothy.
2. **Mix dry ingredients:** In a large bowl, whisk together chestnut flour, all-purpose flour, salt, and rosemary (if using).
3. **Form the dough:** Pour the yeast mixture and olive oil into the dry ingredients. Stir until the dough comes together. Knead the dough on a floured surface for 5-8 minutes, until smooth and elastic.
4. **First rise:** Place the dough in an oiled bowl, cover with a cloth, and let rise for 1-2 hours, or until doubled in size.
5. **Shape and second rise:** Punch down the dough, shape it into a round loaf, and place it on a parchment-lined baking sheet. Let rise for another 30 minutes.
6. **Bake:** Preheat the oven to 375°F (190°C). Bake the bread for 35-40 minutes, or until golden and hollow-sounding when tapped on the bottom.
7. **Cool and serve:** Let cool before slicing.

Maple Cinnamon Rolls

Ingredients for dough:

- 2 cups all-purpose flour
- 1 packet active dry yeast
- 1/2 cup warm milk
- 1/4 cup maple syrup
- 1/4 cup unsalted butter, melted
- 1/2 teaspoon salt
- 1/2 teaspoon ground cinnamon
- 1 large egg

Ingredients for filling:

- 1/4 cup unsalted butter, softened
- 1/2 cup brown sugar
- 1 tablespoon ground cinnamon

Ingredients for icing:

- 1/2 cup powdered sugar
- 2 tablespoons maple syrup
- 1 tablespoon milk

Instructions:

1. **Prepare the dough:** In a bowl, mix warm milk, yeast, and maple syrup. Let sit for 5-10 minutes until bubbly. Add melted butter, salt, cinnamon, and egg, then stir in flour until a dough forms.
2. **Knead the dough:** Turn the dough onto a floured surface and knead for 5-8 minutes. Place in an oiled bowl, cover, and let rise for 1-1.5 hours.
3. **Prepare the filling:** Mix softened butter, brown sugar, and cinnamon in a small bowl.
4. **Roll and fill the dough:** Once the dough has risen, roll it out into a rectangle. Spread the cinnamon filling evenly over the dough, then roll it up tightly.
5. **Slice and bake:** Cut the dough into 8-10 rolls and place them in a greased baking dish. Let rise for 30 minutes, then bake at 350°F (175°C) for 20-25 minutes, until golden brown.
6. **Make the icing:** Whisk together powdered sugar, maple syrup, and milk to make the icing.
7. **Serve:** Drizzle the icing over the warm cinnamon rolls before serving.

Nutmeg and Honey Whole Wheat Bread

Ingredients:

- 2 cups whole wheat flour
- 1 cup all-purpose flour
- 1 teaspoon baking soda
- 1 teaspoon ground nutmeg
- 1 teaspoon salt
- 1/2 cup honey
- 1/2 cup milk
- 1/4 cup water
- 1/4 cup vegetable oil
- 1 large egg

Instructions:

1. **Preheat the oven:** Preheat the oven to 350°F (175°C). Grease and flour a loaf pan.
2. **Mix dry ingredients:** In a bowl, whisk together the whole wheat flour, all-purpose flour, baking soda, nutmeg, and salt.
3. **Combine wet ingredients:** In another bowl, whisk together honey, milk, water, oil, and egg until well combined.
4. **Make the dough:** Add the wet ingredients to the dry ingredients and stir until just combined.
5. **Bake:** Pour the batter into the prepared loaf pan and bake for 40-50 minutes, or until a toothpick inserted into the center comes out clean.
6. **Cool and serve:** Let the bread cool before slicing.

Bourbon-Soaked Fruit Bread

Ingredients:

- 2 cups mixed dried fruit (raisins, currants, apricots, cranberries)
- 1/4 cup bourbon
- 2 cups all-purpose flour
- 1 teaspoon baking powder
- 1 teaspoon ground cinnamon
- 1/2 teaspoon ground nutmeg
- 1/2 teaspoon salt
- 1/2 cup unsalted butter, softened
- 1 cup brown sugar
- 2 large eggs
- 1/2 teaspoon vanilla extract
- 1/2 cup chopped nuts (optional)

Instructions:

1. **Soak the fruit:** Place the dried fruit in a bowl and pour bourbon over it. Let sit for 2 hours or overnight.
2. **Preheat the oven:** Preheat the oven to 350°F (175°C). Grease and flour a loaf pan.
3. Mix dry ingredients: In a bowl, whisk together flour, baking powder, cinnamon, nutmeg, and salt.
4. **Cream the butter and sugar:** In a separate bowl, cream the butter and brown sugar until light. Add eggs, one at a time, beating well after each addition. Stir in vanilla extract.
5. **Combine and fold:** Gradually add the dry ingredients to the wet mixture and mix until just combined. Fold in the soaked fruit and nuts.
6. **Bake:** Pour the batter into the prepared loaf pan and bake for 50-60 minutes, or until a toothpick comes out clean.
7. **Cool and serve:** Let the bread cool before slicing.

Egg-Free Christmas Stollen

Ingredients:

- 3 1/2 cups all-purpose flour
- 1/2 cup sugar
- 2 teaspoons active dry yeast
- 1 teaspoon ground cinnamon
- 1/2 teaspoon ground nutmeg
- 1/2 teaspoon salt
- 1 cup unsweetened applesauce
- 1/2 cup warm water
- 1/4 cup vegetable oil
- 1 teaspoon vanilla extract
- 1 cup dried fruit (raisins, currants, or sultanas)
- 1/2 cup chopped nuts (almonds or walnuts)
- Powdered sugar, for dusting

Instructions:

1. **Prepare the dough**: In a bowl, mix flour, sugar, yeast, cinnamon, nutmeg, and salt. In a separate bowl, combine applesauce, warm water, oil, and vanilla extract.
2. **Mix the dough**: Gradually add the wet ingredients to the dry ingredients, mixing until a dough forms. Knead the dough for 8-10 minutes, adding dried fruit and nuts halfway through.
3. **First rise**: Place dough in a greased bowl, cover, and let rise for 1-2 hours, until doubled in size.
4. **Shape and second rise**: Punch down the dough and shape it into a loaf. Place on a baking sheet and let rise for another hour.
5. **Bake**: Preheat oven to 350°F (175°C). Bake for 30-35 minutes, until golden.
6. **Serve**: Dust with powdered sugar before serving.

Chocolate Chip Babka with Pistachios

Ingredients:

- 3 cups all-purpose flour
- 1/4 cup sugar
- 1 packet active dry yeast
- 1 teaspoon salt
- 1/2 cup warm milk
- 1/2 cup unsalted butter, softened
- 2 large eggs
- 1 teaspoon vanilla extract
- 1 cup semi-sweet chocolate chips
- 1/2 cup pistachios, chopped
- 1 tablespoon honey (for brushing)

Instructions:

1. **Prepare the dough**: In a bowl, combine flour, sugar, yeast, and salt. Add warm milk, butter, eggs, and vanilla extract, mixing until smooth.
2. **Knead the dough**: Knead the dough on a floured surface for 8-10 minutes until elastic. Place in a greased bowl, cover, and let rise for 1-2 hours.
3. **Shape the babka**: Roll dough into a rectangle, spread chocolate chips and pistachios evenly on top, then roll it up tightly. Slice the roll lengthwise and twist the two pieces together.
4. **Second rise**: Place the twisted dough into a greased loaf pan and let rise for 1 hour.
5. **Bake**: Preheat the oven to 350°F (175°C). Bake for 30-35 minutes until golden.
6. **Serve**: Brush with honey for a glossy finish and let cool before serving.

Pumpkin Pecan Bread

Ingredients:

- 2 cups all-purpose flour
- 1 teaspoon baking soda
- 1/2 teaspoon salt
- 1 teaspoon cinnamon
- 1/2 teaspoon nutmeg
- 1/4 teaspoon ground cloves
- 1/2 cup unsalted butter, softened
- 1 cup brown sugar
- 2 large eggs
- 1 1/2 cups canned pumpkin puree
- 1/2 cup chopped pecans

Instructions:

1. **Preheat the oven**: Preheat the oven to 350°F (175°C) and grease a loaf pan.
2. **Prepare the dry ingredients**: In a bowl, mix flour, baking soda, salt, cinnamon, nutmeg, and cloves.
3. **Cream the butter and sugar**: Beat butter and brown sugar until fluffy. Add eggs, one at a time, and then stir in the pumpkin puree.
4. **Combine the wet and dry ingredients**: Gradually add the dry ingredients to the wet mixture until just combined. Fold in chopped pecans.
5. **Bake**: Pour the batter into the loaf pan and bake for 60-65 minutes, until a toothpick comes out clean.
6. **Serve**: Let cool before slicing.

Banana Nut Bread with Bourbon

Ingredients:

- 2 cups all-purpose flour
- 1 teaspoon baking soda
- 1/2 teaspoon salt
- 1/2 teaspoon cinnamon
- 1/2 cup unsalted butter, softened
- 1 cup brown sugar
- 2 large eggs
- 3 ripe bananas, mashed
- 1/4 cup bourbon
- 1 cup chopped walnuts

Instructions:

1. **Preheat the oven**: Preheat the oven to 350°F (175°C) and grease a loaf pan.
2. **Prepare the dry ingredients**: In a bowl, mix flour, baking soda, salt, and cinnamon.
3. **Cream the butter and sugar**: Beat butter and brown sugar until light and fluffy. Add eggs, one at a time, and mix in mashed bananas and bourbon.
4. **Combine the wet and dry ingredients**: Gradually add the dry ingredients to the wet mixture and fold in chopped walnuts.
5. **Bake**: Pour batter into the prepared loaf pan and bake for 55-60 minutes, until golden and a toothpick comes out clean.
6. **Serve**: Cool before slicing.

Holiday Spice Hot Cross Buns

Ingredients:

- 4 cups all-purpose flour
- 1/2 cup sugar
- 1 packet active dry yeast
- 1 teaspoon ground cinnamon
- 1/2 teaspoon ground nutmeg
- 1/2 teaspoon ground allspice
- 1 teaspoon salt
- 1/2 cup warm milk
- 1/2 cup unsalted butter, softened
- 2 large eggs
- 1/2 cup currants or raisins
- 1 egg (for egg wash)
- 1/2 cup powdered sugar (for icing)

Instructions:

1. **Prepare the dough**: In a bowl, combine flour, sugar, yeast, cinnamon, nutmeg, allspice, and salt. Add warm milk, butter, and eggs, mixing to form a dough.
2. **Knead the dough**: Knead the dough for 8-10 minutes. Add currants or raisins and knead until evenly distributed.
3. **First rise**: Place dough in a greased bowl, cover, and let rise for 1-2 hours.
4. **Shape and second rise**: Divide dough into 12 pieces and shape them into buns. Place on a greased baking sheet, cover, and let rise for 1 hour.
5. **Bake**: Preheat oven to 375°F (190°C). Brush buns with egg wash and bake for 15-20 minutes, until golden.
6. **Serve**: Cool slightly, then drizzle with icing made from powdered sugar and a little milk.

White Chocolate Cranberry Loaf

Ingredients:

- 1 1/2 cups all-purpose flour
- 1 teaspoon baking powder
- 1/2 teaspoon baking soda
- 1/2 teaspoon salt
- 1/2 teaspoon ground cinnamon
- 1/2 cup unsalted butter, softened
- 1 cup sugar
- 2 large eggs
- 1 teaspoon vanilla extract
- 1/2 cup buttermilk
- 1 cup dried cranberries
- 1/2 cup white chocolate chips

Instructions:

1. **Preheat the oven:** Preheat the oven to 350°F (175°C). Grease and flour a loaf pan.
2. **Mix dry ingredients:** In a bowl, whisk together the flour, baking powder, baking soda, salt, and cinnamon.
3. **Cream butter and sugar:** In a separate bowl, beat the butter and sugar together until light and fluffy. Add eggs one at a time, mixing well.
4. **Add wet ingredients:** Stir in vanilla extract and buttermilk.
5. **Combine and fold:** Gradually add the dry ingredients to the wet mixture, stirring just until combined. Fold in cranberries and white chocolate chips.
6. **Bake:** Pour the batter into the prepared loaf pan and bake for 50-60 minutes, or until a toothpick inserted into the center comes out clean.
7. **Cool and serve:** Let the bread cool before slicing.

Cinnamon Sugar Pull-Apart Bread

Ingredients for dough:

- 2 1/4 teaspoons active dry yeast
- 3/4 cup warm milk
- 1/4 cup sugar
- 3 cups all-purpose flour
- 1 teaspoon salt
- 1/2 cup unsalted butter, softened
- 2 large eggs

Ingredients for cinnamon sugar filling:

- 1/2 cup sugar
- 1 tablespoon ground cinnamon
- 1/4 cup unsalted butter, melted

Instructions:

1. **Prepare the dough:** In a bowl, combine warm milk, yeast, and sugar. Let sit for 5-10 minutes until frothy. Add flour, salt, butter, and eggs, and mix until a dough forms. Knead on a floured surface for 5-8 minutes, until smooth.
2. **First rise:** Place the dough in an oiled bowl, cover with a cloth, and let rise for 1-2 hours, or until doubled in size.
3. **Prepare the cinnamon sugar:** In a small bowl, mix together sugar and cinnamon.
4. Assemble the bread: Roll the dough out into a rectangle. Brush with melted butter and sprinkle with cinnamon sugar. Cut the dough into strips, then stack the strips and cut into squares. Arrange the squares in a greased loaf pan.
5. **Second rise:** Let the dough rise for 30 minutes.
6. **Bake:** Preheat the oven to 350°F (175°C). Bake the bread for 25-30 minutes, or until golden brown.
7. **Cool and serve:** Allow to cool slightly before serving.

Cranberry Apple Cinnamon Streusel Bread

Ingredients for bread:

- 2 cups all-purpose flour
- 1 teaspoon baking soda
- 1/2 teaspoon ground cinnamon
- 1/2 teaspoon salt
- 1/2 cup unsalted butter, softened
- 3/4 cup sugar
- 2 large eggs
- 1 teaspoon vanilla extract
- 1 cup applesauce
- 1 cup fresh cranberries

Ingredients for streusel topping:

- 1/2 cup all-purpose flour
- 1/2 cup brown sugar
- 1 teaspoon ground cinnamon
- 1/4 cup unsalted butter, cold and cut into cubes

Instructions:

1. **Preheat the oven:** Preheat the oven to 350°F (175°C). Grease and flour a loaf pan.
2. **Mix dry ingredients:** In a bowl, whisk together the flour, baking soda, cinnamon, and salt.
3. **Cream butter and sugar:** In a separate bowl, beat the butter and sugar together until light and fluffy. Add eggs one at a time, mixing well. Stir in vanilla extract and applesauce.
4. **Combine and fold:** Gradually add the dry ingredients to the wet mixture and stir just until combined. Gently fold in cranberries.
5. **Prepare streusel:** In a small bowl, combine flour, brown sugar, cinnamon, and cold butter. Use a pastry cutter or fork to mix until crumbly.
6. **Assemble and bake:** Pour the batter into the prepared loaf pan. Sprinkle the streusel topping over the batter. Bake for 50-60 minutes, or until a toothpick inserted into the center comes out clean.
7. **Cool and serve:** Let the bread cool before slicing.

Pistachio and Apricot Panettone

Ingredients:

- 3 1/2 cups all-purpose flour
- 1/4 cup sugar
- 1/2 teaspoon salt
- 2 teaspoons active dry yeast
- 1/2 cup warm milk
- 1/2 cup unsalted butter, softened
- 3 large eggs
- 1 teaspoon vanilla extract
- 1/2 cup dried apricots, chopped
- 1/2 cup pistachios, chopped
- Zest of 1 orange
- 1/4 cup honey

Instructions:

1. **Prepare the dough:** In a bowl, combine warm milk, yeast, and sugar. Let sit for 5-10 minutes. In another bowl, mix together flour and salt. Add yeast mixture, butter, eggs, and vanilla to the flour mixture, and knead until smooth. Cover and let rise for 1-2 hours.
2. **Add the fruit and nuts:** Once the dough has risen, gently fold in apricots, pistachios, and orange zest.
3. **Second rise:** Shape the dough into a ball and place it in a greased panettone mold or a round cake pan. Let it rise for 1 hour.
4. **Bake:** Preheat the oven to 350°F (175°C). Brush the top with honey and bake for 30-35 minutes, or until golden brown.
5. **Cool and serve:** Let the panettone cool before slicing.

Ginger-Spiced Pear Bread

Ingredients:

- 2 cups all-purpose flour
- 1 teaspoon baking soda
- 1 teaspoon ground ginger
- 1/2 teaspoon ground cinnamon
- 1/4 teaspoon ground cloves
- 1/2 teaspoon salt
- 1/2 cup unsalted butter, softened
- 3/4 cup brown sugar
- 2 large eggs
- 1 1/2 cups pureed pears (about 3 ripe pears)
- 1/2 teaspoon vanilla extract

Instructions:

1. **Preheat the oven:** Preheat the oven to 350°F (175°C). Grease and flour a loaf pan.
2. **Mix dry ingredients:** In a bowl, whisk together flour, baking soda, spices, and salt.
3. **Cream butter and sugar:** In another bowl, beat butter and brown sugar together until light and fluffy. Add eggs, one at a time, mixing well after each.
4. **Add pears and vanilla:** Stir in pear puree and vanilla extract.
5. **Combine and bake:** Gradually add the dry ingredients to the wet mixture and stir until just combined. Pour the batter into the prepared loaf pan and bake for 50-60 minutes, or until a toothpick inserted comes out clean.
6. **Cool and serve:** Let the bread cool before slicing.

Buttery Sweet Potato Bread

Ingredients:

- 1 1/2 cups all-purpose flour
- 1 teaspoon baking powder
- 1 teaspoon baking soda
- 1/2 teaspoon salt
- 1 teaspoon ground cinnamon
- 1/2 teaspoon ground nutmeg
- 1/2 cup unsalted butter, softened
- 1 cup sugar
- 2 large eggs
- 1 cup mashed sweet potato (about 1 medium sweet potato)
- 1 teaspoon vanilla extract

Instructions:

1. **Preheat the oven:** Preheat the oven to 350°F (175°C). Grease and flour a loaf pan.
2. **Mix dry ingredients:** In a bowl, whisk together flour, baking powder, baking soda, salt, cinnamon, and nutmeg.
3. **Cream butter and sugar:** In a separate bowl, beat butter and sugar until light and fluffy. Add eggs, one at a time, mixing well.
4. **Add sweet potato and vanilla:** Stir in the mashed sweet potato and vanilla extract.
5. **Combine and bake:** Gradually add the dry ingredients to the wet mixture and stir until just combined. Pour the batter into the prepared loaf pan and bake for 50-60 minutes, or until a toothpick inserted comes out clean.
6. **Cool and serve:** Allow the bread to cool before slicing.

Red Velvet Pound Cake

Ingredients:

- 2 1/2 cups all-purpose flour
- 1 teaspoon baking powder
- 1/2 teaspoon salt
- 1 teaspoon cocoa powder
- 1 cup unsalted butter, softened
- 1 1/2 cups granulated sugar
- 4 large eggs
- 1 tablespoon red food coloring
- 1 teaspoon vanilla extract
- 1 cup buttermilk
- 1 teaspoon white vinegar
- 1 teaspoon baking soda

Instructions:

1. **Preheat the oven**: Preheat the oven to 350°F (175°C). Grease and flour a loaf pan.
2. **Prepare the dry ingredients**: In a bowl, whisk together flour, baking powder, salt, and cocoa powder.
3. **Cream the butter and sugar**: Beat the butter and sugar until light and fluffy. Add eggs, one at a time, mixing in between.
4. **Add the coloring and flavoring**: Mix in the food coloring, vanilla extract, and vinegar.
5. **Combine wet and dry ingredients**: Gradually add the dry ingredients to the butter mixture, alternating with buttermilk, starting and ending with the dry ingredients.
6. **Bake**: Pour the batter into the prepared pan and bake for 60-70 minutes or until a toothpick comes out clean.
7. **Serve**: Let cool before slicing.

Sweet Sourdough Fruit Loaf

Ingredients:

- 2 cups all-purpose flour
- 1 cup sourdough starter
- 1/4 cup honey
- 1/2 teaspoon ground cinnamon
- 1/2 teaspoon ground nutmeg
- 1 teaspoon vanilla extract
- 1 cup dried fruit (raisins, cranberries, or a mix)
- 1/2 cup chopped walnuts or pecans
- 1 teaspoon salt
- 1/4 cup water (adjust as needed)

Instructions:

1. **Prepare the dough**: In a large bowl, combine flour, cinnamon, nutmeg, and salt. Add sourdough starter, honey, and vanilla extract, then gradually mix in water until the dough is smooth.
2. **Add fruit and nuts**: Fold in the dried fruit and nuts.
3. **First rise**: Cover the bowl and let the dough rise in a warm place for 4-6 hours or overnight.
4. **Shape and second rise**: Punch down the dough, shape it into a loaf, and place it in a greased loaf pan. Let rise for 1-2 hours.
5. **Bake**: Preheat oven to 350°F (175°C). Bake for 30-40 minutes, or until golden and cooked through.
6. **Serve**: Cool before slicing.

Poppy Seed Swiss Roll

Ingredients:

- 1 1/4 cups all-purpose flour
- 1 teaspoon baking powder
- 1/2 teaspoon salt
- 3 large eggs
- 3/4 cup granulated sugar
- 1/4 cup butter, melted
- 1 teaspoon vanilla extract
- 1/2 cup poppy seeds
- 1/2 cup powdered sugar (for dusting)
- 1 cup heavy cream (for filling)

Instructions:

1. **Preheat the oven**: Preheat the oven to 350°F (175°C). Line a jelly roll pan with parchment paper.
2. **Prepare the batter**: In a bowl, whisk together flour, baking powder, and salt. In another bowl, beat eggs and sugar until light. Add melted butter and vanilla extract.
3. **Mix dry and wet ingredients**: Fold the dry ingredients into the wet mixture until smooth. Stir in the poppy seeds.
4. **Bake**: Pour the batter onto the prepared pan and spread evenly. Bake for 10-12 minutes, or until a toothpick comes out clean.
5. **Roll the cake**: While the cake is baking, prepare a clean kitchen towel by dusting it with powdered sugar. Once the cake is done, remove it from the pan and roll it up in the towel while still warm. Let cool.
6. **Prepare the filling**: Whip the heavy cream to soft peaks.
7. **Assemble**: Unroll the cake, spread the whipped cream evenly, then roll it back up. Dust with powdered sugar before serving.

Mulled Wine Bread

Ingredients:

- 2 cups all-purpose flour
- 1 teaspoon baking powder
- 1/2 teaspoon ground cinnamon
- 1/2 teaspoon ground cloves
- 1/4 teaspoon ground nutmeg
- 1/2 teaspoon salt
- 3/4 cup sugar
- 1/2 cup unsweetened applesauce
- 1/2 cup mulled wine (or substitute with red wine and a pinch of spices)
- 1/4 cup vegetable oil
- 1 large egg
- 1/2 cup chopped dried fruit (raisins, apricots, cranberries)

Instructions:

1. **Preheat the oven**: Preheat the oven to 350°F (175°C). Grease a loaf pan.
2. **Prepare the dry ingredients**: In a bowl, combine flour, baking powder, cinnamon, cloves, nutmeg, salt, and sugar.
3. **Prepare the wet ingredients**: In another bowl, whisk together applesauce, mulled wine, oil, and egg.
4. **Combine the wet and dry ingredients**: Add the wet ingredients to the dry ingredients and mix until just combined. Fold in dried fruit.
5. **Bake**: Pour the batter into the prepared loaf pan and bake for 50-60 minutes, or until a toothpick comes out clean.
6. **Serve**: Cool before slicing.

Citrus Walnut Bread

Ingredients:

- 2 1/2 cups all-purpose flour
- 1 teaspoon baking soda
- 1/2 teaspoon salt
- 1 teaspoon ground cinnamon
- 1 cup granulated sugar
- 1/2 cup unsalted butter, softened
- 2 large eggs
- 1/2 cup freshly squeezed orange juice
- Zest of 1 orange
- Zest of 1 lemon
- 1/2 cup chopped walnuts
- 1 teaspoon vanilla extract

Instructions:

1. **Preheat the oven**: Preheat the oven to 350°F (175°C). Grease a loaf pan.
2. **Prepare the dry ingredients**: In a bowl, whisk together flour, baking soda, salt, and cinnamon.
3. **Cream the butter and sugar**: Beat butter and sugar until light and fluffy. Add eggs, one at a time, mixing well between each addition.
4. **Add the wet ingredients**: Mix in orange juice, orange zest, lemon zest, and vanilla extract.
5. **Combine the wet and dry ingredients**: Gradually add the dry ingredients to the wet mixture, mixing until combined. Fold in chopped walnuts.
6. **Bake**: Pour the batter into the loaf pan and bake for 55-60 minutes, or until a toothpick comes out clean.
7. **Serve**: Let cool before slicing.

www.ingramcontent.com/pod-product-compliance
Lightning Source LLC
LaVergne TN
LVHW081500060526
838201LV00056BA/2848